The XXL DAD JOKES BOOK

Hilarious Jokes, Ridiculous Facts and Tongue Twisters that make you Laugh Out Loud

Comedy Sketch Club

Copyright © [2021] [Comedy Sketch Club]

All rights reserved

All rights for this book here presented belong exclusively to the author. Usage or reproduction of the text is forbidden and requires a clear consent of the author in case of expectations.

ISBN - 9798754262782

Contents

5   Introduction to Madness!

9   Question and Answer jokes!

23 Story Jokes

31 *Knock knock*!

53 Terrible Terrifying Torturous Tongue Twisters!

61 The Riddles In The Middle!

69 Fun and Feverish Facts that are Ridiculous, Unbelievable and Insane!

79 Farewell Funny Fellas!

Introduction to Madness!

Welcome one and all to 'The XXL DAD JOKES BOOK'. This book is full of hilarious and hilariously painful jokes, ridiculous facts, and tongue twisters that make you laugh out loud. Not only that, but riddles to trick your friends with, and even a list of Fun and Feverish Facts that are Ridiculous, Unbelievable and Insane!

Have you ever wanted to be the joker? No, not The Joker from Batman, although he would probably find this book just as hilarious as you. No, the joker. The one who for every situation has a hundred jokes at their disposal? The one who has a laugh no matter what? Then you are gonna be the talk of the town once you own this book!

In the question and answer jokes, you will find page after page of hundreds of jokes. Some are new, some are classics - there is a reason why they have stuck around for such a long time, and it's because they have annoyed kids for thousands of years.

They are the kind of jokes your dad tells you thinking that he's funny. But he is funny! These jokes can't stop being funny, no matter how many dads tell them. It is literally impossible.

Not only will this book arm you with hundreds of jokes and make you the joker in your group, but it will also give you a bunch of linguistic tailspins to wrap your taut tongue around in the tongue twister section. You can try these tongue twisters out yourself, on your friends, and especially your parents. See if they can get their heads around these brain-tying, tongue torturing lines of doom! In fact, don't tell anybody, but in this book, there is the most difficult tongue twister of all time. Don't rush ahead looking for it though, because you'll need to build up to it.

Finally, browse through an endless list of some fun and crazy facts that are sure to amaze and entertain anybody in your path, even your teacher. That part comes right after the tongue twisters. Oh yes, you can thank me later on. But for now, I'll just lay it all out on the table for you.

1) Question And Answer Jokes!

2) Story Jokes!

3) *Knock knock* jokes!

4) The Riddles In The Middle

5) Terrible terrifying Torturous Tongue Twisters!

Fun and Feverish Facts that are Ridiculous, Unbelievable, and Insane!

There may only be six sections of this book, but there is a lot of insanity to get through. So let's open her up and split some bloomin' sides!

Question and Answer jokes!

Why did the chicken cross the road?

Yep, we're going there. It's the oldest joke in the book, but the format has existed for a long, long time. All jokes do. Did you know that the oldest joke *ever* can be traced all the way back to 1900 BC? Yep, that's right. And wanna know more? It's a fart joke. That's right. The oldest joke ever recorded has been traced back to ancient Egypt...and it's a fart joke! Wow, that is super duper far back and duper super rude. We've been dead funny for a long time, we humans. Funny as well as clever. And well, the comedy has passed down century after century to get to you. And now, the power has been passed down to you. Congratulations and get ready for some side-splitting giggles!

In this section of the book, you'll find hundreds and hundreds of question and answer jokes. Although we only put one chicken crossing the road joke in there because, well, because there are simply too many chickens to choose from out there for such a joke and we couldn't resist.

And so let's go ahead. I hope you can find a way to enjoy the cringing just as much as the laughter and once you do, you'll be well on the way to giving in to the madness!

Ready, aaaaand...go!

Q: What do you call a bar of chocolate crossed with a man who works with metal?

A: An Aerosmith!

Q: What did one Astronaut say to the other astronaut?

A: I need some space.

Q: What did the jealous boy say to the boy who had all of the toys?

A: Lego that and give it to me!

Q: Why was the shark baffled by the octopus?

A: Because he had so many legs it was like a bite one get one free!

Q: Why did the fish refuse to do the alphabet?

A: Because he was afraid of the C!

Q: Why was 6 afraid of 7?
A: Because 7 murdered 8, 9, 10, 11, and all of the other numbers.

Q: What did the sea say to the beach?
A: It said nothing, but it waved.

Q: How many apples are in a bucket of grapes?
A: A banana this colour. (when telling this one, it helps to hold your arms out to indicate size, for maximum confusion for your friends!)

Q: Why do cheetahs eat before they run?
A: They don't eat. They fast.

Q: What did the egg say to the chef?
A: "Thanks for bringing me out of my shell."

Q: Why did the number 42 go to the dentist?
A: Because he had a forty twooth!

Q: What did the cheese say to itself in the mirror?
A: Halloumi. (Hello me!)

Q: Why did the chicken cross the road?
A: To get away from the KFC on the other side.

Q: What do you call an old woman with superpowers?
A: Supergran!

Q: What do you call Father Christmas in Spain?
A: Tan-ta Clause!

Q: What do you call a fairy without a shower?
A: Stinkabell.

Q: What do you call a house without a chimney?
A: A flat.

Q: Why did the beach turn yellow?
A: Because the seaweed.

Q: What is the strongest part of the ocean?
A: The mussels.

Q: What did the ocean say to the sand?
A: What you dune tonight then?

Q: What is the sleepiest part of the river?
A: The river bed!

Q: What is an astronaut's favourite key on a computer keyboard?
A: The space bar.

Q: Why did the octopus miss the class?
A: Because he was too tenta-cool for school.

Q: Where do Pharaohs like to eat out?
A: Pizza Tut.

Q: Why do people get into the pizza business?
A: To make some dough.

Q: Why did the fizzy drink turn down dessert?
A: Because it was on a diet.

Q: Why did the other fizzy drink cheer?
A: Because it was having a Fanta-stic time!

Q: Why did the third (and final, I promise) fizzy drink rush to the ambulance?
A: To give the patient some lemon aid.

Q: How do you make a can of fizzy drink dance? (I lied, there is one more)
A: Tango!

Q: Why did the Jamaican drink Gatorade? (and one more, but it's Gatorade so it doesn't count!)
A: To get to the finish line Rasta!

Q: There are 47 sheep on the field. The shepherd counts 50. Why?

A: He rounded them up!

Q: Why did both of the fours skip lunch?

A: Because they already had eight!

Q: Why did six obey the rules and behave themselves?

A: So that when it died it could get to seven!

Q: Why did the sheep leave work early?

A: To get to the baaa on time.

Q: What did Ichabod Crane say to the headless horseman?

A: Should have quit while you had a head!

Q: Why did the cows start a band?

A: To make some terrific moosic.

Q: Why was there no time in the office?

A: Because it clocked off early!

Q: What's the similarity between the moon and a dollar?

A: They both have four quarters.

Q: Why did the test tubes break up?

A: Because they had no chemistry!

Q: What did the unicycle say to the tricycle?
A: You are wheely good at this!

Q: What did the basketball say to the pogo stick?
A: Let's bounce.

Q: What is the difference between a guitar and a fish?
A: You can tune a guitar but you can not tuna fish!

Q: What did the big chimney say to the little chimney?
A: You really are too young to smoke.

Q: What did the little chimney say back to the big chimney?
A: Shut up old man, I can do what I want.

Q: What did the big watch hand say to the little watch hand?
A: Don't leave, I'll be back with you in an hour.

Q: What did the digital clock say to the grandfather clock?
A: Look at me, Grandad! No hands!

Q: Why did the girl put the watch on the plane?
A: So that she could watch time fly!

Q: Why did the cats all buy instruments?
A: So that they could make some awesome mewsic.

Q: What did the cows say to their opponents?
A: This really isn't tipping in your favour.

Q: Why did the cows all fall out?
A: Because it wasn't a black and white issue.

Q: What did the cows stop arguing?
A: Because it was a *mooooo*t point.

Q: Why did the cows walk away from the tree?
A: They were waiting for the fruit to fall but it just wasn't apple-ing.

Q: What did the Scottish cat say when it left the party?
A: Al see ya litter!

Q: Why was the orange confused?
A: It had a split personality.

Q: Why wouldn't the banana make friends with the apple?
A: Because it had a seedy personality.

Q: What do you call a bunch of rabbits running away quickly?
A: A receding hare line!

Q: What do you call the fear of being stuck inside a chimney?
A: Santa Claustrophobia.

Q: What do you call a table without any legs?
A: A large plank of wood.

Q: What do you call two mains sockets arguing?
A: A power struggle!

Q: Why is hot faster than cold?
A: Because you can catch a cold.

Q: What is black and white and rolls down a hill?
A: A nun falling down a hill!

Q: What is black and white and goes ha ha ha?
A: The nun who pushed her.

Q: Why did 2 and 2 quit their jobs?
A: They didn't understand what it was all four.

Q: What do you call an octopus without any legs?
A: A squidgy football.

Q: What happened to the joke about the deflated football?
A: It fell flat.

Q: Why did the keyboard leave the party after losing all of his keys?
A: Because he was just board.

Q: Why was the balloon salesman happy all the time?
A: He had an inflated personality.

Q: Why did the puppet leave the tour?
A: There were too many strings attached.

Q: Why did the staple have to give up on the paper?
A: It got too attached to it.

Q: Why did the passengers leave the boat?
A: They weren't on board with it!

Q: What did the car say to the plane?
A: Wow, you just passed us with flying colours.

Q: Why is the difference between ignorance and apathy?
A: I don't know and I don't care! Ha ha ha!

Q: Why are ghosts such terrible liars?
A: Because you can see right through them!

Q: So, what's the issue with glue?
A: Yep, I totally knew you'd get stuck on that one!

Q: What did the leg say to the policeman?
A: "Don't shoot, I won't do you any 'arm!" (get it? Because 'arm?! Eh, eh? Yeah, you get it.)

Q: What did the bee say to the hairdresser?
A: Give me a buzz cut, please.

Q: What is a pirate's favourite letter?
A: Hmm, I don't know. Is it the rrrrr?
A: Actually no, it's the C!

Q: What did the bored clown say?
A: This job really circuses the life out of me.

Q: What was the tornado's favourite board game?
A: Twister!

Q: What do you call a spider on an iPhone?
A: Surfing the web.

Q: Why did the prune take a grape to the dance?
A: Because it didn't have a date!

Q: What did the iron say to the pile of dirty clothes?
A: "You really need to straighten yourselves out."

Q: Why did the biscuit go to the hospital?
A: Because he was feeling crummy.

Q: What did the bus driver say when he drove over a bourbon?
A: "Oh, crumbs!"

Q: Where do wasps go when they're feeling poorly?
A: The Waspital.

Q: Why does Dracula brush his teeth?
A: Because he didn't want bat breath.

Q: Why can you never hear a pterodactyl use the bathroom?
A: Because the P is silent.

Q: Where do cows eat their lunch?
A: In the calf-teria!

Q: Where does a depleted glass of water eat its lunch?
A: In the half-teria!

Q: What did the big pencil say to the broken pencil?
A: "You're pointless."

Q: What did the blunt pencil say to the pencil sharpener?
A: "Get off of me, I'm trying to shave!"

Q: How did the male calculator ask the female calculator out on a date?

A: He just asked for her numbers.

Q: What did the salad say to the man who opened the fridge?

A: "Close the door, I'm dressing!"

Q: Why did the golf clubs walk home?

A: They couldn't find the driver.

Story Jokes

Next to telling jokes, stories have got to be one of the oldest things in human history! We humans have always loved a good story! Nothing is better than sitting down and listening as someone else tells you a story, and says something clever and witty while they do so! Story jokes can be brief or they can go on for a bit. Sometimes, people will play a joke on you by making the story long and then when they reach the end, you realise that the punchline is awful, if it could even be called a punchline! Story jokes can include a riddle or they can have a song. But one thing that binds them together is that you must be alert for them to work, even if they are absolutely terrible. Because one way or another, you have to be ready for the punchline at the end. In this chapter, you will find jokes of all kinds. Some of the jokes in this segment are like this. They require you to soak in the details but are all for fun and games in the end.

Well, nothing kills a joke more than trying to explain it, so let's just dive on in and get our sides splitting. Or cringing, which is just as likely, but either way, there's something to report to the person sitting next to you by the end of it!

1. I went to a wedding the other day and I'll tell you what, it was a really emotional one. Even the cake was in tiers!

2. I heard that the planet Earth is over 70% water, and most of the sea bed is sponge. Can you even imagine how much water there be on the planet if you took the sponges out?!

3. The other day I looked everywhere and couldn't find my stress ball - I got frustrated and angry because I couldn't find it!

4. Those *Knock knock* jokes are so brilliant that whoever invented them should get the Nobel prize.

5. So there's a man in a bar. The barman comes up to him and says, "Would you like a drink?" and the man says "Okay, sure," and so the barman gets him a drink. The man then drinks it, and then the barman comes back again, offering him another. "Okay, sure," the man says, and the barman pours him another drink. After the second drink, the barman comes back a third time and offers the man a *third* drink. "I probably shouldn't with what I've got," says the man.

6. "What have you got?" asks the barman.

7. "50p," the man says.

8. I think it's totally possible to land on the sun. You just have to go at night.

9. Did you know that there is a world record out there for most watches eaten in three minutes? The man who holds the record today ate a total of three and a half watches in that amount of time...that's truly incredible, but not necessarily in a good way. But one thing I'm confused about is this: *But how did they time him?!*

10. The large man got fired from his job at the bakery because of his *attitude*, and when I first heard about it I thought that he had actually eaten somebody's hat!

11. You don't hear many good jokes about steak lately. Rare, aren't they?

12. Okay fair enough, that was a great steak joke. Wait for it, wait for it...I want to congratulate you on your amazing stek joke...Well done!

13. The best thing about numbers is that you can always count on them.

14. I am worried about calendars. Their days are numbered.

15. Frodo was very surprised one day to wake up in his home in The Shire only to find a gigantic Tesco in the middle of Hobbiton. In all of his adventures and dreams, he had never prepared for this. It certainly was an unexpected item in the Baggins area.

16. So, when I was at school, I knew three boys named Zack, William, and Peter, but everyone called them Zip, Willy, and P. These names were so well known that even the teacher called them by these names. But they were little troublemakers too. One day before the teacher arrived, it was chaos. Zack was jumping around on the table, William was hiding in the storage cupboard, and Peter was throwing paint around the classroom. When the teacher walked in and saw the chaos she was furious. She yelled, "Zip - DOWN. Willy - OUT. P - IN THE CORNER!"

17. Three boys arrived at a park, a park that they came to often. But something was different this time. There was a magical slide there and a mystical figure told them all that when they go down it, whatever word they say on the way down will be given to them when they land. This was exciting news. When the first boy went down the slide he cried out for "Gold!", and when he whizzed to the bottom of the slide, it was a pile of gold that he landed in. When the second boy went down he too wanted to ask for gold, but thought better of it and simply cried out, "Money!" and landed in a pile of fifty-pound notes adding up to a great sum of money. When the third boy reached the top of the slide, he looked down at the slide. He wasn't interested in things like gold and money, because he knew that these things would not make him happy in the long run. He was the kind of boy who simply enjoyed things, and so he decided that this would be no different. Rather than wishing for anything he decided to just enjoy the ride. He put his legs on the slide, pushed himself down - and it was the best, most fun slide he had ever gone down. The joy of it was so great that he

cried out, "Weeeeeeeeee!"...and he landed...yeah, you know where he landed.

18. Three football fans and a camel were lost in the desert. One of the fans supported Liverpool, another Hartlepool, and the third Arsenal. They loved their teams so much that they based many of their life decisions on their teams. After a great many hours walking through the desert they got so hungry that they decided to eat their camel. It was their only choice in the hot desert. They couldn't decide how to eat the camel and so they stuck to their teams. "I'm Liverpool, so I'll take the liver," said the Liverpool fan. "Well I'm Hartlepool, so I'll take the heart," said the Hartlepool supporter. The Arsenal fan hesitated and said, "I'm not hungry."

A warning must be given before we unveil this next joke because it is just so ridiculous! And long, but trust me, it will be worth it! Also, it's great for your friends, because you can make a joke on them, by making the joke last as long as you want to make it! This is the Joke About A Purple Man.

19. One day in Purple Town, a purple man woke up in his purple bed to the sound of his purple alarm clock going off. The purple man looked at the time and realised that he was late for his purple work, and so he jumped out of his purple bed, threw on some purple clothes, and then went to get in his purple car. He turned his purple keys in the purple car and reversed out of his purple drive and then drove down the purple road. He was so late for purple work that he drove above the purple speed limit. It wasn't long until the purple policeman caught on that the purple man was speeding, and then pretty purple soon after that the purple man heard the purple police sirens going off like this:

PURR-PLE! PURR-PLE! PURR-PLE! PURR-PLE! And so the purple man pulled over to the side of the purple road and waited for the purple policeman to come to the window, and the purple policeman was in a particularly purple mood, and so he ordered the purple man to get out of his purple car. The purple police officer put handcuffs on the purple man and took him to the purple police car, and then drove the purple man all the way to the purple police station. The purple policeman took the purple man out of the purple car, brought him into the purple police station, and walked him down to the purple police cells. The purple policeman opened a door on one of the purple police cells and said, "Right then mate - indigo!"

20. A woman got on an airplane with a pram and sat down. The man sitting across from her turned, looked at her. His eyes widened and he said, "Oh dear, lady. That has simply got to be the ugliest baby I ever did see." The woman is furious and she leaps up and yells across the train for the conductor, who shows up in a hurry. "Sir," she said to the conductor, "This man has just offended me." The conductor looked at her and said, "I really do apologize, Ms. I heard the whole thing and it was not the kind of thing we tolerate on this train! I'll have a word with him in just a moment but for now, please just come along with me and I'll find you a great seat in the first-class bit — and not only that but I'll find you a nice sack of nuts for your monkey."

21. Two women are driving, and they get into an accident. They climb out of their cars and one says to the other, "Wow! I can't believe we survived that. We should celebrate by having a drink." "Yes, we should!" says the other woman, so thrilled by the fact that she has

survived the ordeal. The first woman goes to her car and brings out a bottle of wine and pours two glasses, handing one to the other woman, who drinks it. "Good health!" she says after she has drunk it. When she realises that the other woman hasn't drunk hers, she asks her why, and she replies: "I think I'll just wait until the police arrive before I drink mine."

22. **(This is a very long joke with a very weak punchline. You have been warned)** In a small town far from here, where it was constantly Halloween, bad things kept happening. A skeleton told the town that there would be a meteor strike one night, but they all laughed at him. "Whatever, Skelly!" they all said. But just hours later, rocks flew through the atmosphere. A year later, the skeleton told everyone that there would be a flood, and again, they laughed. But not quite as hard this time. "Okay, Skelly," they said. "You were right last time but that was purely by chance, I'll bet." But just hours later, the town flooded! A year later the skeleton told the town that soon there would be a vampire attack, and they laughed at him once again. "Skelly, this is getting silly. Just because you got it right the last couple of times, doesn't mean that you are right again this time. Now shove off." But just hours later that night, vampires attacked the town. This time, the mayor of the town got involved. He went up to the skeleton and asked him just how on earth he had managed to predict that such bad things were about to happen, so often and so accurately. The skeleton shrugged and said, "I could just feel it in my bones."

23. A military plane was about to crash. The pilot and the sergeant were panicking. The plane was too heavy. To solve the problem, they decided that they would throw some items out of the plane, and hopefully, that would put them right. So they threw the three heaviest items out of the plane: a toolbox, a keg of water, and a bomb. Lo and behold, this sorted them out. The plane leveled out again and all was well. When they landed the plane and walked around, the pilot and the sergeant happened across a boy who was crying. They asked him what was wrong and the boy told them that a metal box had fallen from the sky and hit him on the head. Next, they came across a girl, who was also crying. She was also soaking wet. She told them that out of nowhere, she had been struck by water. The next boy that the pilot and the sergeant came across was a boy, and he was laughing harder than they had ever seen a boy laugh before. When they asked him what he was finding so very funny, he said; "I farted and a house blew up."

Knock knock!

Knock-knock jokes go back to the dinosaur times, and are still classics. That's not true, about the dinosaurs, but it wouldn't be too hard to believe, would it!? Even considering that there were no such things as doors back then. In actual fact, the knock-knock joke might have come from Shakespeare. In Macbeth, you'll see it there. That is one theory anyway. But we don't know the answer to everything, and what does it matter. For better or worse, knock-knock jokes are a thing. In fact, there is no worse about it at all! It's just a good thing! Some things are just around and we don't know why! Like doorknobs, or skirting boards. Knock-knock jokes are like that except they're a bit more fun!

Below you'll find some of the classic ones as well as some brand new ones, all of which are always great to try out on your friends and your parents. What's that? Have you heard anything? No way, I heard it too. It sounded like...I mean, it almost sounded like someone was at the door...

Knock knock!

Who's there??

Beak.

Beak who?

Please will you beak quiet?

Knock knock!

Who's there??

Turnit.

Turnit who?

Turn it off!

Knock knock!

Who's there??

Orange.

Orange who?

Orange you glad there are a bunch more of these awful *Knock knock* jokes to come?

Knock knock!

Who's there??

A little old lady.

A little old lady who?

I didn't know you could yodel!

Knock knock!

Who's there??

Cash.

Cash who?

Fair enough but I prefer walnuts.

Knock knock!

Who's there??

Water.

Water who?

Water you standing there for, are you not gonna let me in?!

Knock knock!

Who's there??

Hi ho.

Hi ho who?

All right, there's no need to make silly noises.

Knock knock!

Who's there??

Twit.

Twit who?

Crikey, you've turned into an owl!

Knock knock!

Who's there??

Ding dong!.

Ding dong who?

Don't mess about. If you're gonna have a doorbell, at least answer the door when I ring it!

Knock knock!

Who's there??

Louder bell.

Louder bell who?

As in, get a louder bell. Now. I'm sick of waiting for you to answer the door!

Knock knock!

Who's there??

Fish.

Fish who?

God bless you!

Knock knock!

Who's there??

Wheely...

Wheely who?

I'm having a wheely good time!

Knock knock!

Who's there??

Quiche.

Quiche who?

Just gimme the quiche and I'll open this door myself!

Knock knock

Who's there??

Sea.

Sea who?

No Seagull, you nitwit!

Knock knock

Who's there??

Est

Est who?

Estuary.

Knock knock

Who's there??

Cart.

Cart who?

Me too, I love cartoons!

Knock knock

Who's there??

Horton.

Horton who?

Horton hears a who?

Knock knock!

Who's there??

Boom boom.

Boom boom who?

Well if that's not gonna get your attention I don't know what is!

Knock knock

Who's there??

Theresa.

Theresa who?

Theresa green.

Knock knock

Who's there??

Pizza

Pizza who?

Pizza good guy.

**Knock knock*

Who's there??

Apple.

Apple who?

**Knock knock*

Who's there??

Apple!

Apple who?

Knock knock

Who's there??

Apple.

Apple who?

Knock knock

Who's there??

Orange.

Orange who?

Orange you glad I didn't say apple again?

Knock knock

Who's there??

Bow.

Bow who?

Bow tie.

Knock knock
Who's there??
Justin
Justin who?
Justin time!

Knock knock
Who's there??
Damver.
Damver who?
Actually, it's pronounced Hoover Dam!

Knock knock
Who's there??
Taco.
Taco who?
It's time taco!

Knock knock
Who's there??
Come on, ketchup.
Come on ketchup who?
Come on, ketchup with me!

Knock knock

Who's there??

Boo.

Boo who?

There there now, there's no need to get upset!

Knock knock

Who's there??

Swing me.

Swing me who?

Swing me a song!

Knock knock

Who's there??

Tension.

Tension who?

Ten shuns and you're out!

Knock knock!

Who's there??

Woo.

Woo who?

Well, I'm glad you're having a good time cos I'm not.

Knock knock

Who's there??

Police.

Police who?

Police stop knocking on my door!

Knock knock

Who's there??

Yaa.

Yaa who?

Not for me. I actually prefer to use Google!

Knock knock

Who's there??

Car.

Car who?

Bet ya car tell who's knocking at your door!

Knock knock

Who's there??

Tin.

Tin who?

Open the door, I'm still wait tin!

Knock knock

Who's there??

Fidgeting.

Fidgeting who?

Don't be fidgeting who you are!

Knock knock

Who's there??

Task.

Task who?

I'll buy it for'tasking price!

Knock knock

Who's there??

Nose.

Nose who?

Who nose how long these jokes could go on for?

Knock knock

Who's there??

Cargo.

Cargo who?

Nope, car go vrum vrum.

Knock knock

Who's there??

Penguin

Penguin who?

The pen thief is making all the penguin fast!

Knock knock

Who's there??

How now.

How now who?

How now brown cow.

Knock knock

Who's there??

Eaty.

Eaty who?

Eaty go home.

Knock knock

Who's there??

Figs

Figs who?

Figs the doorbell, it's broken!

Knock knock
Who's there??
Lettuce
Lettuce who?
Lettuce in before I freeze to death!

Knock knock
Who's there??
Aneta.
Aneta who?
Aneta borrow a pen!

Knock knock
Who's there??
Howard.
Howard who?
Howard I know?

Knock knock
Who's there??
Just Joe.
Just Joe who?
Just joking around with you!

Knock knock

Who's there??

Elena

Elena who?

Stay in Elena we'll have no problems!

Knock knock

Who's there??

Hugh.

Hugh who?

Hugh do you think you are??

Knock knock

Who's there??

Mons.

Mons who?

Where!?

Knock knock

Who's there??

Mine.

Mine who?

Mine your own business!

Knock knock

Who's there??

Jess

Jess who?

Jess watch where you're going will you?

Knock knock

Who's there??

Nobody.

Nobody who?

...

...

...

(when you do this one for your friends, be silent when they say 'nobody who?')

Knock knock

Who's there??

Doctor

Doctor who?

Yep, that's right.

Knock knock

Who's there??

Juno.

Juno who?

Juno how funny I am?

Knock knock

Who's there??

Amglad.

Amglad who?

Amglad you're still reading this book.

Knock knock

Who's there??

Brrrrrrr.

Brrrrrrrr who?

It's brrrrr freezing out here, just let me in!

Knock knock

Who's there??

Mice

Mice who?

Mice to meet you!

Knock knock

Who's there??

Watts.

Watts who?

Watts gotten into you?

Knock knock!
Who's there??
Abey.
Abey who?
singing Abey C D E F G...

Knock knock
Who's there??
Cat.
Cat who?
Cat got your tongue?

Knock knock!
Who's there??
Inuff.
Inuff who?
Inuff with the terrible jokes!

Knock knock!
Who's there??
I am app.
I am app who?
You definitely are.

Knock knock!

Who's there??

Stayway.

Stayway who?

Stayway from me!

Knock knock!

Who's there??

Windsor.

Windsor who?

Windsor bad!

Knock knock!

Who's there??

A really impatient cow.

A really impatient cow wh...

MOOOOOOOOO!

Knock knock

Who's there??

A really, really, *really* impatient chicken.

A really...

BAWWWWWWWWWK!!

Knock knock

Who's there??

Radio.

Radio who?

Radio not, here I come!

Knock knock

Who's there??

You.

You who?

Yoo hoo, anybody in?

Knock knock

Who's there??

Rough rough.

Rough rough who?

Did somebody let the dogs out? Cos I can hear barking!

Knock knock

Who's there??

Spell.

Spell who?

Double you, aitch, oh.

Knock knock

Who's there??

Tree.

Tree who?

Treat me with respect and answer the bloomin door!

Knock knock

Who's there??

Surely.

Surely who?

Surely you're having the time of your life with these awesome(ful) jokes?

Knock knock

Who's there??

Alex plain.

Alex plain who?

Alex plain it all to you later, but for now, LET ME IN.

Knock knock

Who's there??

Twit.

Twit who?

Twitter is my favourite social media platform.

Knock knock

Who's there??

Meme.

Meme who?

No need to be meme to me. ANSWER THE DOOR ALREADY!

Knock knock

Who's there??

Font.

Font who?

Sounds delicious, have you got any bread to dunk in it?

Knock knock

Who's there??

Goat.

Goat who?

Goat to the supermarket and get some shopping.

Knock knock!

Who's there??

Best.

Best who?

Best you stop making jokes and let me in now.

Knock knock!

Who's there??

Envy.

Envy who?

I envy you, all warm inside while I'm freezing at this door!

Terrible Terrifying Torturous Tongue Twisters!

Now, who in their right mind would invent these things? Sentences that confuse the brain and make us feel all silly while everyone laughs at us! Well, it's not *all* about that. Did you know that when we practice tongue twisters over and over and over again it actually improves our elocution? That means that they help us talk better. It's true. When we learn to pronounce tricky sounds and phrases, it helps us speak clearly, loudly, and intently! That's the benefit of them...but yes, that doesn't make them any more frustrating and tongue-tying! But if you try them over and over again you will find that you get better at them. That they really do help you to pronounce things well. Or sing, if that's your thing. Or to do amazing speeches. Yep, these terrible tongue-twisty thingamabobs are actually useful in many ways. Who'd have known!

But they're not all terrible. Some of them are simple, in fact, many of the first ones are pretty easy to do. Find one that you find difficult and practice it...but maybe after trying some of the easier ones first, and not after too many fizzy drinks! But try and pronounce all of the letters clearly and become the best speaker in the world!

Some of these are written down multiple times. Two reasons for this. One, to make you read it aloud multiple times, and also to make you read it in your head multiple times. Some of these aren't just tongue twisters, but brain twisters as well! Some of them might not make a heck of a lot of sense, but that's what makes them so fun to do! Let's go. Try not to lose too many brain cells in the process!

1. The terrible truth tastes like toothpaste. The terrible truth tastes like toothpaste. The terrible truth tastes like toothpaste.
   (with this one it's all about the first R. Get that loud and clear and you're on the right track..to Hell!)

2. The dentist didn't do the dishes.

3. The broomstick stood still in a stilton storage station.

4. Some biscuit caskets caught a cumbersome cucumber. Some biscuit caskets caught a cumbersome cucumber. Some biscuit caskets caught a cumbersome cucumber.

5. How many bicycles could Miley Cyrus cycle if Miley Cyrus could cycle in Cyprus?

6. How much cud could a cold cow chew if a cold cow could chew cud?

7. How much hair would a bear wear and tear if a bear would tear hair he wears?

8. How much weather would a weather man weather if a weather man could weather weather?
    And now I give to you, dear reader, the most tricky, torturous tongue twister ever devised by man...

9. Pad kid poured curd pulled cod.
    (Try that one on for size!)

10. Sixty-nine Neptune ceilings sing to Nanny. Sixty-nine Neptune ceilings sing to Nanny. Sixty-nine Neptune ceilings sing to Nanny.
    (try that one really fast and watch your tongue get confused as heck!)
    Four boys brought flour four boys brought flour four boys brought flour.

11. Green lorry orange lorry green lorry orange lorry green lorry orange lorry.
    (just as effective as red lorry yellow lorry)

12. How can a clam cram in a clean cream can? (x10 really fast!)

13. I wish to wash my Irish wristwatch (x10 really fast!)

14. Settle the shell in the shop. Settle the shell in the shop. Settle the shell in the shop.

15. Trey the truncheon taught tools in the trench. Trey the truncheon taught tools in the trench. Trey the truncheon taught tools in the trench.

16. Ten million moaning lilies. (x infinity super fast!)

17. Beckon the bread for your breakfast. Beckon the bread for your breakfast. Beckon the bread for your breakfast.

18. Red lolly yellow lolly red lolly yellow lolly red lolly yellow lolly.

19. A proper pot of coffee from a proper copper coffee pot. Proper pot of coffee from a proper copper coffee pot.

20. I like unique New York. I like unique New York.

21. I wish to wash my hands in a warm water hole (x3)

22. I tried to list the turnips in the time that they turned up. I tried to list the turnips in the time that they turned up. I tried to list the turnips in the time that they turned up.

23. Betty Botter bought a bit of butter, but the butter that she bought was a bit bitter, so Betty Botter bought a bit of better butter.

24. When you bite the double bubble gum bubbles always double.

25. Perry poked a proper penguin with his pencil, but the penguin pecked Perry back particularly pointedly and Perry felt the pain.

26. Tina told her toddler that her toys were terrible. Tina told her toddler that her toys were terrible. Tina told her toddler that her toys were terrible.

27. Bernard brought his iced bun to the border of Iceland. Bernard brought his iced bun to the border of Iceland. Bernard brought his iced bun to the border of Iceland.

28. Kelly kicked the cat when the kittens clawed her hat.

29. Clive caught a carrot in a callous can of coke.

30. Greek grapes Greek grapes Greek grapes.

31. Train a chin to chew on shoes. Train a chin to chew on shoes. Train a chin to chew on shoes.

32. She sees green cheese she sees green cheese she sees green cheese.

33. Billy's big bunny blundered by the bobble brush. Billy's big bunny blundered by the bobble brush. Billy's big bunny blundered by the bobble brush.

34. Terry taught a towel terrific tricks.

35. Granny got gherkins from Dorothy Perkins.

36. Stephen stopped at ten train stations. Stephen stopped at ten train stations. Stephen stopped at ten train stations.

37. Eight echelons ate EpiPens in the epicenter of America. Eight echelons ate EpiPens in the epicenter of America. Eight echelons ate EpiPens in the epicenter of America.

38. Fuzzy Wuzzy was a bear. Fuzzy Wuzzy had no hair. So he wasn't fuzzy wuzzy, was he?

39. If a chihuahua chews on checkered shoes, which checkered shoes does he choose?

40. She slit the sheet, and on the sleet, she sat, and the slitted sheet is my seat.

41. I thought I had a thought, but the thought I thought was not the thought I thought. So if the thought I thought was not the thought I thought then why did I think I thought it?

42. How can a scam cram a cracker in a green can when the cracker cram scam is a cracker of a con.

43. If you carefully cross a crossing where the cows are crossly crossing then your course should be of course to not cross the crossing cows.

44. Ronald ran to Rhonda Ronald ran to Rhonda Ronald ran to Rhonda.

45. Timmy trapped a tepid tortoise inside a television, but the tortoise taught Timmy that the cruelty was not his mission, so Timmy took the tepid tortoise out of the television.

46. Shea sharpened shandy with the shavings of a shiv.

47. Michael Manning made a mess with a molten man of metal, and the molten mess he made was made with many metals. So Michael Manning made a mannequin to make his mess a mission, and Michael managed afterward to mend the mess he made.

48. Callum caught a kitten in the corner with a kettle.

49. Eleven elevated Elvis elves.

50. William wondered whether the weather would be wintery, but whether the weather was wintry or the weather was hot, William had to weather it whether it was cold or hot.

51. The little beetle bit the big bug, but the big bug bit the beetle back.

52. Mr. See had a saw, and Mr. Soar had to see it. So Mr. Soar went to see See and took a look at See's saw. Mr. Soar touched the saw and it made him very sore, so Mr. Soar saw Mr. See no more.

53. What noise annoys a toy soldier? No noise annoys a toy soldier, I told ya!

The Riddles In The Middle!

Have you ever wanted to amuse and bemuse your friends by asking them a question and then seeing them try and answer it? Meanwhile, you know the answer! We all have. And so with that said, here are a bunch of riddles you can try on your friends. Riddles too, go back a long time. And they go back all the way to the Greeks. Ah, those Greeks. It's always them, isn't it? They were a clever bunch of buggers, those Greeks!

Some riddles leave out information to make us guess in the wrong areas, while some just use word play to twist our heads the wrong way. Whichever it is, riddles get us thinking and help our brains remember stuff! It's true, just like the tongue twisters, riddles are good for you.

With these, try and get them before going on to read the answer. They're good for you to do, not just to trick and fool your friends with. Although, of course you can do that afterwards!

Remember what I said about The Joker earlier? Well, I'll be damned, this is probably the point where you *can* become The Joker from Batman!

Q: If it takes an entire day to dig a hole, how long would it take to dig half of a hole?
A: You can't dig half a hole!

Q: If there are two ducks in front of a duck, and two ducks behind a duck, and a duck in the middle, then how many ducks are there in total?
A: Three!

(How? Because all of the ducks mentioned are the same ducks. It's like if we put three dots down on a page like this:

. . .

There are two dots behind a dot, two dots in front of a dot, and a dot in the middle!)

Q: A plane crashes on the border of America and Canada. Where do you bury the survivors?
A: You don't bury survivors!

Q: There are twenty sick sheep on a farm and one dies. How many are there?
(This is all about how you pronounce it. You must say it quickly so that whoever is listening hears the words ' twenty-six sheep' rather than what you

actually say, which is 'twenty sick sheep'! And the answer of course is...)

A: Nineteen.

Q: There is a donkey with a rope around its neck, and a basket full of carrots a few meters away from him. How will the donkey reach the carrots?

A: Easily. The other end of the rope isn't tied to anything!

Q: A woman goes down a one-way street, and the police see it, but don't bat an eye. How come?

A: She was WALKING down the road!

Q: A rich family lived inside a large and circular-shaped cottage. They had a servant, a housemaid, and a lawnmower. One day, the mum and the dad went away, and so before they left they sent them to bed and said goodbye for the night. But when they came home again, later on, the children had all disappeared. The parents searched the circular house and soon discovered that they had been abducted! The police arrived and asked the servant, the housemaid, and then the gardener what they were up to when the abduction happened. The servant said he was folding clothes, the housemaid said she was dusting the corners, and the gardener said he was cutting the grass. Which one of them is telling fibs? And which of them abducted the kids?

A: The housemaid did it, and is lying. Why? Because she said that when the kidnapping happened, she was dusting the corners, and at the beginning, I said that the rich family lived inside a circular-shaped cottage! Oof, I bet that one got you for a while! Or maybe you just read the answer straight away...hopefully you didn't!)

Q: What can you see in the water that never, ever gets wet?
A: The reflections.

Q: My home is orange. The walls are orange, the floor is orange, and the walls are orange. The fridge is orange, the oven is orange, and the oranges are very, very orange indeed. Even the bananas are orange. Woah! So, what colour are the stairs?
A: Wait for it...there are no stairs. I live in a flat!

Q: There are three apples on the apple tree. You take away two of them. How many apples are you left with?

A: You have two apples!

Q: What has hands and a face, but no legs, nose, or ears?

A: A clock!

Q: Brendan's mother has three kids. Two of them are named Ed and Edd. What is the third one named?

A: Brendan! (this is Brendan's mother we're talking about, at the end of the day!)

Q: What word becomes long when you take two letters off of it?

A: The word 'longer'!

Q: What word becomes short when you take two letters off of it? (spoiler alert!)

A: The word, 'shorter'!

Q: How high can you jump? Can you jump higher than a house?

A: Of course you can not jump higher than a house. A house can't jump!

Q: Dracula can't see himself in the mirror. He can look into a mirror but he can't see himself there. And so why is his hair always so neat?

A: I genuinely have no answer for this one.

Q: If three is company and four is a crowd, what is four and five and six?
A: Fifteen!

Q: What food do you have to break in order to make?
A: An egg!

Q: What happens once in a lifetime, twice in a moment, but never in a thousand years?
A: The letter M!

Q: I have four legs but can not run. What am I?
A: A table.

Q: What is black and white, and read all over? (This makes more sense when you say it aloud).
A: A newspaper!

Q: A girl and a doctor are sitting together. The girl is the doctor's daughter but the doctor is not the girl's mum. How?
A: The doctor is the girl's father!

Q: What is black and white and when you kick it, it flies in the air?
A: A football.

Q: I can make you speak like an Indian.

A: How?

A: See, I've already got you going.

Try this one on your friends
Take a piece of paper or a pencil (Something small anyway, could be a tennis ball, doesn't matter) and tell them there is a rule when handing it back and forth. Then pass it to them and say "This piece of paper (or pencil or tennis ball) is..." and name something beginning with the first letter of their name. Say their name is Matthew, say, "This piece of paper is a magazine." You can pass it back and forth for hours before your poor friend figures it out!
Extremely Hard Riddle Alert!

Q: The land of Ogg has one rule. Can you guess what it is?

In the land of Ogg, you can have glass but you can not have windows. You can have feet but you can not have legs. You can not have light, day, night, or dark, but you *can* have darkness. You can have sheep but you can *not* have lambs. You can have wool and cotton but you can *not* have clothes. You can not have eyes, but you *can* see. You can not have a nose, but you *can* smell. You can look, but you can *not* touch.

What is the one rule of Ogg?

I'll give you a minute.

...

...

...

A: Time for answers! In the land of Ogg, you can have anything that has the same two letters together. Glass. Feet. Darkness. But not windows, legs, or night. Told you it was a hard one!

Fun and Feverish Facts that are Ridiculous, Unbelievable and Insane!

Here we are. After those terrible elocution lessons it's fitting to end with some gentle funny and/or interesting facts. Did you know that having the ability to recite random facts makes you look super smart? Not only that, but although the facts that you read might seem useless at the time, the chance to show it off comes up more than you know when you read the fact! Plus, they're just fun to read. But you'll now realise that after reading this book, as well as being the funniest dude in the school, you will also be the cleverest. Funny and clever. That's something to be proud of! And so with that said, here is a list of Fun Feverish Facts that are Ridiculous, Unbelievable and Insane! Just try not to remember all of them or there will be no space in your brain left! Just kidding.

Interesting Facts

1. Did you know that a crocodile cannot stick its own tongue out?

2. Did you know that the nose can pick up on a trillion *different* smells?

3. Did you know that it is humanly impossible to lick your own elbow?

4. Did you know that four is the only number with the same amount of letters as the number?

5. Did you know that the colour of octopus blood is blue and they have nine brains? They must be super clever, eh?

6. Did you know that the universe is 14 billion years old? That's one thousand million for every billion, so 14 thousand million years! That's a whole bunch of time!

7. Did you know that it's humanly impossible to sneeze with your eyes open? Don't go trying that one out now!

8. Did you know that crisps make us put on weight more than any other food in existence?

9. Did you know that it is humanly impossible to hold your nose and hum at the same time?

10. Did you know that it is possible to be able to hold a note forever? This is done by breathing both inwards and outwards! Which is a skill hard learned, but a skill nonetheless!

11. Did you know that reaching the speed of light is technically achievable, but a human being couldn't survive the speed?!

12. Did you know that cockroaches have been around since dinosaur times?

13. Did you know that dogs are so smart that they can *smell* illness?!

14. Did you know that without a nose and saliva we wouldn't be able to taste anything?

15. Did you know that rats are loved and adored and respected in some countries?

16. Did you know that bogies are just water combined with protein?

17. Did you know that itching is a form of pain?

18. Did you know that your own eyes can tell the difference between about ten million colours? They're like the nose of the eyes.

19. Did you know that over the course of a year you blink 4 and a half million times?

20. Did you know that the goo inside your eyeball stays in the same place for your entire life?

21. Did you know that the dinosaurs lived on the planet earth for about 165 million years? Compared to humans who have only been around for about 200 thousand years. Woah!

22. Did you know that some dinosaurs lived up to 300 years? In theory anyway, because being a dinosaur, life could be pretty violent and you might not make it that long anyway!

23. Did you know that there are some parts of the sea that are so deep that the sun doesn't reach them? It's called The Midnight Zone. The sea goes pretty bloomin' deep!

24. Did you know that the fastest gust of wind that has ever been recorded in human history is 253 miles per hour? That's so fast that it would blow you away!

25. Did you know that if the world stopped rotating for just a second, every object on earth would be flung into the air at an unbelievable speed? Yikes, don't think about that one too much, that's some scary stuff!

26. Did you know that the first computer ever was invented in 1833 and that it took over forty years to develop? Woah, thanks a lot to whoever did that! (Charles Babbage)

27. Did you know that if everybody on the planet jumped at the exact same time...nothing whatsoever could happen because of how big the earth is?!

28. Did you know that if there was no such thing as spiders, within two earth weeks there would be a ball of insects as big as the earth? Thank God for spiders, and that you don't have to wear protective gear everytime you leave the house!

29. Did you know that in Hawaii you can see rainbows the size of mountains?

30. Did you know that snails can sleep for three years?

31. Did you know that caterpillars have twelve eyes? Imagine all the things you could see as a caterpillar!

32. Did you know that sharks are the only fish in existence that can blink using both of its eyes?

33. Did you know that tigers don't just have striped furs, but striped skin too? That's why they're oh so stripey!

34. Did you know that owls can turn their heads almost 360 degrees (that's the whole way round) without bursting blood vessels or breaking their necks? It would feel super weird to be an owl!

35. Did you know that for every grain of sand on the planet there are 10,000 stars? There are roughly about seven quintillion, five hundred quadrillion grains of sand on earth. I suddenly feel very small.

36. Did you know that there are about 2,000 thunder storms on earth every single minute?

37. Did you know that 1 single bolt of lightning is 5x hotter than the sun? The sun is often 27 million degrees Fahrenheit.

38. Did you know that worms can tell when a flood is coming? They're kinda smart, actually. That's why they wiggle up to the surface when the water's coming!

39. Did you know that it would take a thousand years to fly to Pluto in a maximum speed airplane?

40. Did you know that the biggest mammal on the planet is the blue whale, which has an average size of 80 feet, and weighs about 150 tonnes? That is about 20 buses or 15 houses.

41. Did you know that the tallest building in the world is the Burj Khalifa and it is almost a thousand metres tall?

Funny Facts

1. Did you know that the word that means 'fear of long words' is...*wipes forehead*...here we go...hippopotomonstrosesquippedaliophobia? That might be the scariest word in existence!

2. Did you know that it is technically possible to become a zombie? It's true. There is a state that humans can go into that is very similar to that of a movie zombie!

3. Did you know that the original name for Uranus was George?

4. Did you know that peanut oil can be used to create dynamite?!

5. Did you know that the technical term for a blob of toothpaste is a 'nurdle'?!

6. Did you know that even though owls can turn their heads almost 360 degrees, they can't move their eyes? That explains it, then. It's give and take when you're an owl.

7. Did you know that "zwieback" is a form of biscuit eaten in Russia?!

8. Did you know that the colour orange is called orange because of the fruit? By this logic, the colour of yellow should be called banana.

9. Did you know that statistically speaking you are twice as likely to be killed by a vending machine than a shark?!

10. Did you know that when we go up in an airplane our taste buds are not as good as when we are on the ground? Next time you hear someone complaining about airline food, tell them that!

11. Did you know that because of moving tectonic plates, India could technically disappear over a long period of time? This is because the moving plates push the mountains an inch or two higher a year and that the weather also knocks an inch or two off the mountains!

12. Did you know that if you bang your head against a wall a couple of hours a day, it actually burns a significant amount of calories?! It also might make you pretty stupid, so don't go trying that out!

13. Did you know that if you put grapes in the microwaves (Greek grapes Greek grapes Greek grapes) they will explode?

14. Did you know that human beings are the only species on earth with chins? That is doubly true for those with double chins.

15. Did you know that in many countries, being fat is considered a good thing?

16. Did you know that in medieval times, having a pale face was a sign of importance, because it meant that you stayed indoors? The servants were tanned because they did the gardening and the chores! It's the opposite way around today! Brown is good now. Strange world!

17. Did you know that in 1947 the first living creatures were sent into space...and they were fruit flies!?

18. Did you know that in Scotland there are over 400 words for 'snow'? Must be mighty cold over there and in so many different ways!

19. Did you know that apples are a fourth water? This explains why everyone is always 'bobbing for apples' at fairs!

Farewell Funny Fellas!

I hope that you enjoyed the facts as well as the funnies! That's about it for us. It's time to put some of those terrible or terribly funny jokes to good use, just as much as the fantastic facts and the painfully torturous tongue twisters. Have good practice, and see if you can make a few of your friends laugh, as well as give them something to think about...or in the least case, just give them a tongue tying test try on for size!

Remember, humour is healthy and fun, and a little bit of both of those a day can't hurt us. So long!

Disclaimer

This book contains opinions and ideas of the author and is meant to teach the reader informative and helpful knowledge while due care should be taken by the user in the application of the information provided. The instructions and strategies are possibly not right for every reader and there is no guarantee that they work for everyone. Using this book and implementing the information/recipes therein contained is explicitly your own responsibility and risk. This work with all its contents, does not guarantee correctness, completion, quality or correctness of the provided information. Misinformation or misprints cannot be completely eliminated.

Printed in Great Britain
by Amazon